==The Must Have, Do-This-Then-That, Seller Dialogue Cheat Sheet for Every Real Estate Investor==

The Secret To Seller Negotiations Most Investors Will Never Know About...And Your Competition Hopes You Never Discover

Discover Motivated Sellers (Faster), Reveal Their Pain Points (Easier) and Lead Them Down The Path of Profitability Without Conflict, Resistance or Opposition (Automatically)

A Free Report
By Erik Stark

www.TheRealErikStark.com
Instagram.com/TheErikStark
Facebook.com/TheErikStark
www.RealEstateWhileYouDrive.com
www.EriksFreeBook.com

DISCLAIMER: No Part of This Publication May Be Reproduced or Transmitted In Any Form , By Any Means - Mechanical or Electronic, Including Photocopying or Recording or by Any Information Storage and Retrieval System Without Written Permission From The Publisher. Requests for Permission or Further Information Should Be Addressed to Erik Stark

Erik Stark
Erik@TheRealErikStark.com

You may download your digital copy of this report at https://therealerikstark.com/site/wp-content/uploads/2018/09/The-Secret-to-Negoating-FINAL-DRAFT.pdf for additional resources and live links.

Before you sit down to make your next batch of seller phone calls or launch your campaign with expectancy of receiving live calls, practice these dialogues with your team or spouse (or a complete stranger if you have to) and learn how to lead sellers down the path of success and take them from where they are to where they want to be in the shortest time, with the least amount of hassle.

This is the same timeline my partner Steve Mills and I have used for the past several hundred deals.

Some Will. Some Wont. So What. Someones Waiting.

While even the most well constructed sales process wont convert 100% of its customers, by practicing these dialogues, learning the language that all human behavior responds to, knowing how to respond proactively to rejections and understanding what words to NEVER use, you will have increased your chances for success 10x.

I will give tremendous credit to the mentors in my life that have helped me create a systematic approach to buying more real estate.

First and foremost my business partner Steve Mills who is an incredible visionary that never will leave well enough alone and has alongside chiseling away at this dream of being real estate entrepreneurs. And for Greg Pinneo and Mike Cantu who have been mavericks in my life, helping create a platform of all that we can be.

For you, I am grateful.

I now pass the buck onto you. We're in this together.

Erik Stark

Pre Set to Taking/Making Phone Calls

Be In Your Zone - When Taking/Making Seller Calls, If You're Consumed Or Frustrated, Let It Go To Your Voicemail....Hopefully Your Voicemail is A Secure Call Capture Process That Begins Your Unique Seller Experience. DO NOT JEOPARDIZE Your Next Payday If You Are Not Prepared to Give Your Seller The Experience That Has Proven To Work More Effectively Than Just Shooting From The Hip.

Tune Into WIIFM - Unfortunately, No One Cares About You, And As Much As We Might Care , We Are Here For The Money (That Leads To Freedom). The Way to Freedom Is To Provide Relief To Peoples Situations In Exchange for Compensation. You Can Eliminate Most Of Your Resistance By Listening For Their Pain Points and Give Them Options To Relief As Quickly As Possible. Get In The Habit of Making Sellers Feel Understood and Let Them Feel The Confidence of Your Ability to Help. Talking About How Great You Are, Deals You Have Done, Does Not Move Their Meter At All.

Know Your Ultimate Goal - The Goal of My Phone Calls Is NOT To Close The Deal. Its To Get The Face to Face Meeting Which Is Where I Close Almost 100% of My Meetings. Especially With a Incredible Follow Up Process. If The Phone Call Doesn't Go Well, They Go Into My Follow Up System. Unless I Truly Feel That I Can Change The Direction of Our Conversation By Meeting In Person, I Typically Just Leave Them With A Good Feeling About Our Conversation to Open The Door Later On and Revisit The Opportunity. REMEMBER. You Are 10x More Likely To Do Business With Someone Who You Have Spoken To Before Than You Are With a Brand New Client.

Know Their Name, Ask for Permission to Use it and Use It Often - People Are Terrible With Names. Your Sellers Included. Yet Everyone Loves to Hear Their Name. Use it Correctly. Us it Often. Just Don't Be Obnoxious and Use It Obviously.

Get Them To Laugh - This Is Usually My Que That We Have Made A Connection. I Want Sellers To Look At Me As Someone Who Is Helping Them Get From Where They Are To Where They Want To Be. Not Someone Who Is Here To Take Their Equity. If You Can Break The Barrier Of Getting Them To Drop Their Guard And Laugh With You, Its A Pretty Clear Indication That You Have Moved Your Status To Friendship Level Vs Client.

NEVER Make an Offer Without Making A Connection - This May Be My Most Passionate Point With Sellers. It May Only Take 10 Minutes To Get Here, It May Not Be Until Our Third Conversation, Yet I DO NOT MAKE AN OFFER UNLESS I MAKE THE CONNECTION.

I Get Ridiculous Calls From Sellers Who Say "Well You Mailed Me So Tell Me What Your Paying and Ill Tell You If Its Worth My Time". This Is A Clear Indication We Have Someone In La La Land and If You Want to Lose Them, Just Give A Number and They'll Hang Up.

My Typical Response Is "Sir, You Wouldn't Respect Me As a Professional If I Just Blurted Out A Number. That Would Be Like Walking Into A Dealership To Buy A Car And Just Shouting A Number The Moment You Walk In".

You Have To Understand The Idiots These People Deal With. The "UNvestors" Who Have Absolutely No Agenda or Logic To Their Principles of Negotiation.

Leave Your Ego Outside Your Office and Bite Your Tongue As Much As You Just Want to Shut These People Down. This Is Why You Excel When Most Others Fail.

Seller Call Reference Card

- Get In The Zone Before Picking Up The Phone
    1. Go Walk
    2. Go Psyche Yourself Up
    3. Focus On Breathing and Remove Your Frustration
    4. Whatever It Takes. Find Out How To Get Yourself In Your Zone
- What Their Favorite Station To Listen To? _____
    1. Where Are They Now?
    2. Where Are They Trying To Go?
    3. Show Them The Road Map You Have To Get Them There...
- What Is My Goal With This Phone Call? _____
    1. Identify Pain Points
    2. Determine The Level Of Motivation
    3. Discover How You Will Lead Them Down The Path To Fruition
- What Is Their Name? _____
    1. Ask Permission to Use It
    2. Use It Often
- Get Them To Laugh
    1. Life Experiences
    2. Past Seller Situations
    3. Anything To Connect Personally and Share A Laugh
- Never Make An Offer Without Making A Connection
    1. Kill Your Ego
    2. Find A Way To Relate
    3. Open Them Up
    4. Let Them Vent About Life While You Lead Them Down YOUR Path To Results

Drag This Image To Your Desktop and Print of Few Off To Use Before You Make Your Next Calls (Ive Also Included A Few At The End of This Report)

Seller Dialogue:

This is how my conversation goes with a seller. Its been put to use so much that it flows natural and there is no robo questions coming through. That makes the seller feel as if they are dealing with someone who knows exactly how to lead this conversation down the path to fruition...

"Hello This is Erik, You Have My Full Attention. How May I Help You?"

SELLER: Hi Erik, My name is Cathy. You sent me a letter about my property.

"Hi Cathy. Thank you for taking the time to contact me today. Do you have a few moments for us to chat about the property?" (I ALWAYS ASK FOR SELLERS PERMISSION TO TALK)

SELLER: Yes. Thats why I called.

"Perfect. Do you have any questions for me before we begin"?

SELLER: Yes! How did you find out about my property since its not listed for sale?

"GREAT Question Cathy. So we don't generally buy properties that are listed for sale with real estate agents. We prefer to buy them directly from the property owners since

we have found that sellers often want a different outcome than Realtors typically offer. So we took a trip to the assessors office to see who has owned property for a while in the neighborhood and we send a few letters out to see if they are interested in selling! Pretty interesting right?

(I often slip something in at the end to get them to agree with me. Creating a "yes" state allows you to direct the flow of the conversation and getting your sellers to agree with you makes it easier to control the conversation as you build more rapport).

SELLER: Yes, very interesting. I receive a lot of letters and postcards about my property but something about yours seemed different.

Well thank you for that Cathy. Would mind telling me what seemed different?

SELLER: Its just that your envelope looked different. Like it was written personally for me. I've also received several letters from you over the years so I guess I noticed your still buying. Most other letters come once and I never hear from them again. The letter was also very genuine and personal to my situation.

It feels great to hear what you are telling me Cathy. We strive to stay active in our community and let people know we are humans too that are simply looking to buy more property.

Alright... so what can you tell me about the property?"

This whole process is just to get them acclimated to opening up and vent about whats really going on. Let them tell the story. Get the background to help you understand. Listen for motivation and ultimately get them comfortable to ask more serious questions determining just how motivated they are.

The conversation should remain very genuine and casual. Keep in mind the goal is to extract the pain points and reveal motivation. Don't EVER be authoritative, belittling or "above" your sellers.

Sometimes you will need to ask a few questions or one question a few different ways to get them to open up.

If you find they are still not revealing too much use a variation of these questions and look for every situation to connect with them, get them laughing and make them feel as if you are talking like close friends would.

Can you give me a little background on the property?

What is the current situation with the property?

Can you give me a general idea of the condition of the property?

Are you aware of any city violations or outstanding issues with the property?

When was the last time the property was occupied?

What are you looking to accomplish with the sale?

Is this an investment for you?

What would you ideally like to see happen with the property?

Any other family members who are helping you decide?

Are you looking for all cash or are you interested in continuing to receive a secured monthly income stream?
(I like to slip this question in very last and say it in this exact order to open the door for potential owner finance discussions. By asking them about cash first and leaving off with owner finance it piques curiosity and begins the opportunity to discuss)

Listen for pain points that you can provide relief to.
Once, AND ONLY ONCE you have got them to open up you can begin asking the real questions that get you to real progress. Sellers and I often talk for 5+ minutes just letting them release all that they need to get out about the property. Once they know you are not a threat, you will hear life stories unfold, pain points repeat, how their brothers cat ruined their whole summer and a host of other tell tale signs that they are comfortable with you.

Once I feel we have made significant advancements in them being comfortable with me and I have determined some forms of motivation and pain points, I will begin to ask questions that get us to the root of us doing business...Keep in mind, this is totally casual and like to humans conversing back and forth.

"So Cathy, Do You Have An Overall Idea Of What <u>You Feel</u> The Property is Worth?"
This is MUCH different than asking them what they want. Your simply putting feelers out there to get them to identify if they have a good our poor idea of values in the area.

"So Cathy, Do You Have An Overall Idea Of What <u>You Feel</u> The Property is Worth?"

THEN SHUT UP AND LET THEM RANT AGAIN...

Once they are done

"How Did You Come Up With That Number?"
This is Important to know, that way you can determine if they are in reality or la la land. Are they truly aware of values in their area or are they apart of the heresy crowd that knows more than the local experts? Then you can begin leading them down the path to success by giving them the simple breakdown of working from the market value backward to give authentic justification as to why your number is what it is...

If I believe they are WAY OFF, I will position the question like

"Oh wow. Im having a hard time supporting that number. Where did you come up with that amount"?

Let them tell you where they came up with the number...and then casually ask

"If The Price is Right, Are You Willing to Move Forward And Open Escrow?"
This simple question of proposition determines whether you have someone snooping or is truly ready to sign when you meet.

It is so crucial to have them meet you at the correct value. Done right, there is no way to cheat the process of beginning at the end value and working backwards towards a fair offer.

As you will see as we move on, getting them to agree on back end price allows you to have their validation on final sale price, general price of repairs needed and costs associated with the sale.

Done causally and without greed, most sellers quickly realize that you are well educated on the local market and what it takes to get this deal done.

Heres my follow up question again...

"If The Price is Right, Are You Willing to Move Forward?"

SELLER: Yes. Im ready to sell if the price is right...

"Are You Looking For All Cash or Would You be Interested in Receiving a Secured Monthly Interest Income From He Sale of The Property?"

This one question has opened up more opportunity to buy owner finance deals than our owner finance marketing ever generated. Learn to ask this question with confidence and be sure to offer cash first and leave them with them the finance option second that way it sits in their mind. By offering cash first and financing second, you psychologically placed the load on the seller finance portion of the offer.

SELLER: That sounds interesting. Id like to find out more and how that works.

"Very Well. When Would Be a Good Time For Us to Meet at the Property?
Once you have discovered you have a true motivated seller, you simply do what you know how to do best. The goal is to meet, build further rapport and then once you have truly reconnected, take control of the conversation and casually bring it back on track.

Rarely does it ever happen, however once in a while a seller will want a general offer before they are willing to have us come over. I recite my conversation from the beginning of the book and say **"well Cathy, its truly tough to be accurate on my price without knowing what I am bidding on and I feel as if I am doing you a disservice by giving you an offer without seeing your property"**.

SELLER: I understand. Do you have a general idea?

"I can only go based on recent sales but if properties are selling for $150k. Factoring our general $60 per square foot renovation costs, we would be somewhere between $50,000 and $75,000".

I always restate the reasoning behind my offer so they can feel the proof of my ballpark price.

Typically I try to hold off on prices until I have visited the property.

Many times when we meet in person and have been doing a good job of making a connection, I often say things like **"Goodness Cathy, We Have Been Chatting Like Old Friends for Quite A While I Almost Forgot While I Was Here".**

Then I begin constructing the foundation for the educated offer where we can prove to them the market value and begin walking backwards towards our offer.

From the after repaired value, working backwards, here is how the offer and conversation goes. (Again, we do not ever begin to switch our conversation back to the property and our offer until we feel that they are totally comfortable with us).

"We Both Agree That Your Property is Worth $150,000 Once its Fixed Up in Top Condition, Right?"

Seller: Yes

The comps prove that to be true. We are not dancing around that. Get the seller to agree with you as you go along. This is where the "yes" state begins to work in your favor now.

*Side Note - When I bring comps, I discount the highest and discount the lowest. I am not trying to bank on top dollar for a sale, however if it happens, its cream on the top. I am also not trying to low ball and buy for what a few properties that may have been bought at a very great price.

The goal is a fair deal and to buy at fair market value.

Then I walk through two scenarios

One is what they can expect to sell the property for if it was fixed up in top condition, sold through a realtor, to a first time home buyer, while vacant.

This paints the picture of what we are going to have to go through in order to get a little pay day at the end and in almost every scenario, they come to reality that they do not want to be the ones in this position doing all this work for a "potential" bit more money.

The other is working backwards from that sale price of $150,000 to show justification as to why our offer is for 50%-80% of what its worth. Yes we still pay 80% of market value on some properties. When you operate in A class neighborhoods, you will not be buying quality real estate for 50 cents on the dollar. You may occasionally, yet not enough to sustain real growth.

Here is how you begin to craft your educated offer.

After Repairs Sale Price minus Itemized Repairs minus 10% Buffer for Problems minus 10% Sales Cost minus Small Margin Left Over For Us To Hopefully Retire to A Small Fishing Village One Day Equals The Offer Price.

  After Repair Sale Price ($150,000)
- Roof ($8000)
- Kitchen ($10,000)
- Landscape ($2000)
- Floors, Doors, Fixtures and Trim ($2500)
- Bathroom ($4500)
- Windows ($7000)
- Total $34,000
- 10% Buffer ($3500)
- 10% Sales Cost on $150,000 (Commission 6%, Title 2%, Taxes 2%) $15,000
- Margin (Our goal is a 30% margin because there are always cost/time over runs and especially if you are assigning properties, you need cushion for your assignment fee and your buyers profit from rehab. Our 30% margin is based off of the ARV-Repairs-Buffer-Sales Cost. If you try to base it off your sale price, you will have really got a bargain on the house and that may be a great starting point, however you may wind up at 30% of your acquisition and repair cost total combined number.
-   Margin ($150k - $34k - $3.5k - $15k = $97,500 x 30% = $29,250)

Offer Price $68,250

Once you lay this out, and especially once you have perfected it, there really is no real objection for them to give other than illogic, irrational or greed.

Again, getting the seller to agree on back end sale price, cost of the repairs and sales costs lines them up to receive your offer price much more easily than just throwing out your final number.

Don't forget that the greed can also be found in your margin and occasionally this is an area you know you may likely have to reduce your margin.

Realistically, we work as many buffers in as we can for the simple reason that there will be intense negotiations, there will be cost over runs on projects, the project always goes over budget, over time, insurance, holding costs, utilities, property tax, income tax, payroll tax not to mention the agent requests and ridiculous buyer requests when it comes time to sell, appraisals, agent compliance fees, the endless hours you spend managing contractors, gas. The list is endless.

This is not to create a phony buffer but it is the stark reality of what we deal with on a daily basis and rarely do projected profits end up being what was originally intended.

Its at this point that you can occasionally lose the sellers interest because the offer is slightly less than they thought.

If that is the case, you can bring it back into control by helping them see the value in what is required to get top dollar for their property. They can go capture the $29,250 themselves if they want to round up contractors and learn what buyers want and how to design kitchens and all the talent we bring as investors.

Depending on how well your relationship is with them at this point, I occasionally give them the opportunity to remind them that they are more than welcome to take my position and go through all the hassles and leg work (reminding them its a challenge to those who have a platform and a team, let alone those who don't)...**or they can pick up their check in the next 7 days.**

Don't be afraid to walk away from the deal, yet do it subtly by letting them know that when you walk away, they have to begin this process all over. I usually remind them that we are also actual buyers. The other post cards they have are from wholesalers who truly don't have much logic when it comes to crafting offers and therefore give the industry its "low baller" name.

This can also be a good time to revisit why they called us vs the others. Often times we find out in our conversation that they did in fact reach out to other investors. Generally, they didn't answer or just gave the seller such a combative phone conversation that the seller never needed to have them come out.

I can tell you from my personal experience that most sellers are driven more by relief of a burden than they are for money. We have case study after case study to prove it. Keep cool and get them over the fence.

You can also offer to pay their closing costs as an incentive to your negotiation. It only costs you a few thousand extra and gets their mind working around a net number. Depending on what state you are in and depending when taxes are due, it may be in your favor to tell the seller you will pay all closing costs and write in the actual net number of the sale price write in the additional terms and conditions. In our states, we generally benefit here because the seller has paid their taxes in advance and by giving them a net amount, it allows us not to have to reimburse their tax prorations. Again, an additional buffer of negotiation.

I might say

"So Cathy, it looks like we are not far off. What if I agree to pay all your closing costs and you walk away with $70,000? Can we agree to let me pay the closing costs and move this forward?"

If I feel I am about to lose a seller, Ill change the topic. Get them talking and laughing again. Then once you have opened them back up and get them to see the light in a different perspective.

Is she willing to wait 6 months for the additional $29,000?

What I do is divide the $29,000 margin by 6 (months it will take her to get it) and come up with $4,833.33, then I divide again into 30 (days in each month) and come up with $161.11 and then reaffirm your question...

"Cathy, do you realize we are only $161.11 per day away from moving this forward? Id really like to get my team on this property (never use the word deal) and Im quite sure you're looking forward to picking up your check in the next 7 days and getting this behind you..."

Most importantly, I advise all our mastermind students to WRITE THE OFFER. I don't care if they already have it "sold", are listing with their agent or whatever they are trying to tell you.

Write the offer, get it in there hand and reconfirm that they are willing to take on the process of going after all equity in the property themselves.

If they still don't want to commit, all you can do at this point is get the number that works for them and begin rearranging your margins and buffers to determine if you have a deal that makes sense.

There have been times, both to my advantage and disadvantage where I met with the seller and brought a fully written up purchase agreement, and we would sit at the table and I would have the seller fill in their price.

Usually its more than I would offer. Occasionally it was way less than I was offering.

If you master this process and timeline, you will be so far ahead of your competitors and truly get a sense of having a Unique Seller Experience where you can become the expert in getting these sellers to the closing table. You have to put in the work. Get to your 10,000 hours as quickly as possible.

The key points to making this successful are to be genuine and authentic. Use the sellers name. Get them to laugh. Determine pain points. Reveal motivation. Create a "yes" state. Get them to agree every time they throw you an objection and you respond. Get them to "approve" and agree on the pricing you mention. Be fair. Listen to their needs. Connect with them.

Below is a seller reference card for you use as your guide before you get on your phone calls.

Go to the conversation above and recite this over and over until it becomes a casual conversation. I often say "uh, ah, so, yeah, hmmm, really"...and normal words that are part of a normal conversation. It gives depth to my character to know I am not a scripted robot.

Seller Call Reference Card

- Get In The Zone Before Picking Up The Phone
    1. Go Walk
    2. Go Psyche Yourself Up
    3. Focus On Breathing and Remove Your Frustration
    4. Whatever It Takes. Find Out How To Get Yourself In Your Zone

- What Their Favorite Station To Listen To? _____
    1. Where Are They Now?
    2. Where Are They Trying To Go?
    3. Show Them The Road Map You Have To Get Them There...

- What Is My Goal With This Phone Call? _____
    1. Identify Pain Points
    2. Determine The Level Of Motivation
    3. Discover How You Will Lead Them Down The Path To Fruition

- What Is Their Name? _____
    1. Ask Permission to Use It
    2. Use It Often

- Get Them To Laugh
    1. Life Experiences
    2. Past Seller Situations
    3. Anything To Connect Personally and Share A Laugh

- Never Make An Offer Without Making A Connection
    1. Kill Your Ego
    2. Find A Way To Relate
    3. Open Them Up
    4. Let Them Vent About Life While You Lead Them Down YOUR Path To Results

9 Words to NEVER Use When Talking With A Seller

I am stupefied when I hear how so many investors talk. I call so many bandit signs around town, call all the mailers that the sellers give us when we buy their property. I can't imagine anyone ever taking a deal down the way I hear some people talk, let alone get to the point of buying properties in A class neighborhoods.

Here are some common words I hear people say all the time that you should never use and the words you should replace them with. You literally need to remove these from your vocabulary when talking with sellers.

Investor - Use the word builder, property owner or property buyer. Use handyman with a hammer if you need to. ANYTHING but investor. Those guys are right up with car salesmen.

Fast Cash - Try to move away from being a fast cash buyer. I have never met a seller who truly needs cash in three days and this usually scares them. Take it slow and push for the owner financing. If they want all cash, I still paint the picture that this will be settled in about 30 days although if they need it sooner, then we make it happen. Just begin moving yourself away from being the fast cash guys. In the savvy world of A class neighborhoods, fast cash means you're an amateur.

Profit - Use the word margin. Most people understand you need to have a margin for yourself. No wants to be profited from.

Wholesale - Use And/Or Assigns. If they ever ask what this means, tell them its a protection clause that allows you to bring in a partner in the event you get hit by a bus but generally means you just have not determined which company name it will go into.

Qualify - I once heard an investor say they need to qualify them before they meet. My mouth dropped. Instead of qualifying, I use the word discover.

Execute The Contract - Seriously? Who wants to be executed? Tell them we need to "ok the agreement".

Steal - Get comfortable with the language of a fair market value. The definition of fair market value is the price a buyer and seller agree upon.

Offer - Instead of writing an offer, tell them you will be drafting a proposal. Proposals are harmless. Offers open up the door for the seller to receive more offers.

Home - Use the word property. Do not use house, home or anything that inspires emotional triggers.

Common Objections

Seller: "Oh no, I wont accept that low of a price"

Me: "I understand your position. What will you accept"?
This allows them to feel understood by you (vs telling them how stupid and greedy they are) and puts the situation right back in their hands.

Seller: "I don't want to waste time so if you plan to give me a low ball offer, don't bother"

Me: "GREAT, because we pay fair market value for all our properties. I will include a copy of the recent sales in your area comparable to your property along with a detailed breakdown of how I arrive at my offer price. Would that be ok for you?"
I can give reference to several properties we have bought way under what the competition was offering because our positioning was greater and our ability to educate and walk them through this with authenticity and professionalism is way easier for them to internalize than the guy who walks through and tells them how crappy the property is and how much work it needs. Show them what fair market means. Educate them. It generally replaces the low ball simply because you are showing how you arrived at the fair market, low ball offer.

Seller: "What happens if you don't move forward or don't give me the money"?

Me: "Great question. In rare situations, we have had to release ourselves from moving forward and that typically means the acquisition and repair cost are more than what the margin is worth. So unless you have us in a position where we are really trying to figure out how our numbers will work, there really is no reason for us not to move forward. However, since this is all being done through a licensed title company, if we don't do business, you are free to sell your property to anyone you like. Seem fair"

This takes the pressure off you and puts it right back in there hands and even tells them, the only way we don't move forward is if we are not making money.

I hope this report gave you some mentality clarity or at least a baseline to begin indirectly negotiating like a pro.

Its not going to be perfected overnight. You may stumble over your words occasionally and possibly lose a deal or two, however I assure you that with repetition and a sincere conversation you will close more deals and make sellers feel great about giving you a testimonial.

Practice these often with coworkers and team members.

This is just the beginning of a new path and getting your 10,000 hours starts now. It may help to break this down onto index cards so you can compartmentalize your conversations and increase your lead conversion.

Remember, nothing works if you don't.

Thank you for spending the time to educate yourself and increase your knowledge. Our industry desperately needs exceptional people who still do business with integrity and authenticity.

Until we speak again. I am grateful you chose to spend this time with me.

Sincerely,

Erik Stark

Did you enjoy this free report? This is just one of the many strategies we discuss in our annual mastermind and with our one on one coaching students.

If you would like more information about how to increase your lead flow, improve your lead conversion, learn how to maximize your deals, make big money with small lists and simply do bigger deals with less headache and live the real estate investor lifestyle, here are five simple ways to get the laser focus of investors who have walked the path before you and can show you a few ideas that worked well for us and are guaranteed to give you great results.

Get Featured On Our Podcast - We are delighted to have special guests on our podcasts that are willing to share whats working for them and this call also doubles as a "business detox session" where we will give you several ideas and strategies that you can implement in your business immediately. Simply go to www.RealEstateWhileYouDrive.com/Give-back

Al La Carte - Do you have a pretty good handle on your real estate business yet could use some occasional guidance, motivation or negotiation strategies? We offer the opportunity for one hour focused time blocks to discuss your current situation or opportunity. These calls are based on your specific needs and can be used at your discretion. Call requests are usually set up within 48 hours. Email request can be sent to Erik@TheRealErikStark.com

Annual Mastermind - Are you looking to be a part of a small group of investors that have figured out whats really working? We work with a small group of investors throughout the year. Typically less than 15 at a time simply because we still run a full time business and there is a lot of work that goes into creating content and action plans for those who want to get to the next level. This is not open for new investors. You must be operating a minimum six figure annual business. Register for our next mastermind right here. (www.SelfManagingFreedom.com)

One on One - There is no one size fits all glove that will teach you real estate. Truth is no coach can help anyone if they don't know where they need the help. Work with US (not some assigned coach) to hone your skills, determine target markets, create marketing pieces that stick, learn how to convert sellers, increase property values, understand zoning, how to assign for larger paydays (our smallest assignment in the last 3 years was $25,000, up to $85,000). We can take you from where you are to where you want to go. You must be operating a minimum six figure annual business. Six month commitment (although most stick with us for a few years leaving few openings to join) Apply For One on One Monthly Education Right Here.

For more case studies forms, downloads, reports, mind maps and free resources you can use right now to make money in your business just visit http://therealerikstark.com/resources/

ERIK STARK

Erik Stark is an Expert Real Estate Entrepreneur, Educator, Marketer, Uber-cool Dad and Dedicated Husband of 14+ Years.

Erik has purchased hundreds of properties, created masterful marketing pieces, shared the stage with the top real estate and personal development educators, helped thousands of people improve their lives and continues to pour his life into people, friendships, disciplines, breakthroughs and growth.

Here Are Some of The Remarkable Achievements of Erik Stark

- Assigned his first deal at age 24
- Purchased over 400+ properties since including single and multi family, apartments, commercial, vacant land, family portfolios and developments
- Raised millions of dollars in private capital for acquisitions
  Studied and created some of the industries greatest marketing pieces
- Helped dozens of investors do their first deal
- Invested over $150,000 into his education
- Has spent well over 10,000 hours in the field of real estate acquisition, finance, negotiation, management and development
- Coached for several top real estate educators
- Created unique operating platforms the deliver consistent, dependable results
- Featured as the "underground expert" in numerous online communities
- Turned his house flipping hobby into a brick and mortar company with his business partner Steven Mills by age 26
- Acquired $1,000,000 in real estate equity by age 30
- Runs a local young professional mens ministry near his home in South Florida
- Active member of the community supporting Habitat for Humanity, Sheridan House Ministry and Homeless Voice
- Dedicated Father who supports his sons passion for exotic cars (@SoFlaSuperCars)
- Committed man of 14+ years to his lovely wife who supports his sacrifice, breakthroughs, appreciation for great living and constant and never ending improvement of life.

Erik Specializes In:

- Marketing and Innovation
- Deal Structuring
- Raising Private Capital
- Owner Financing
- Negotiation
- Making Big Money With Small Lists
- Street Level Investing

Eriks Top Interview Questions:

- What is the single best advice you can give to any investor?
- What were the biggest breakthroughs in your business?
- How did you transition from wholesaling to building wealth?
- Where do you find motivation for pursuing your passion?
- What is a typical day for Erik?

Learn More About Erik at www.TheRealErikStark.com

Become Friends With Erik Online

www.facebook.com/theerikstark/
www.twitter.com/theerikstark
www.linkedin.com/in/theerikstark/
www.instagram.com/theerikstark/
www.instagram.com/realestatehacks/

Author:
How To Buy Your First Real Estate Property:
An Uncommon Approach To Finding Hidden, Competition Free Properties In Any Market

The Essential Textbook for New and Experienced Real Estate Investors!

www.EriksFreeBook.com

You Can Make It Happen. We Believe In You.

Erik@TheRealErikStark.com

www.ingramcontent.com/pod-product-compliance
Lightning Source LLC
Chambersburg PA
CBHW041303180526
45172CB00003B/954